THE STORY OF JESUS
BIBLE STORIES
OF THE NEW TESTAMENT

Cover Design by
Lance Raichert and Paul E. Nunn

Illustrated by Shaun M. Venish
Printed in the United States. All rights reserved.
Copyright 2002.

Published by
Pyramid Publishing
P.O. Box 129
Zenda, Wisconsin 53196

The Angel Gabriel told Mary that she would give birth to the Son of God.

Mary and her husband Joseph went to Bethlehem to be registered for the census.

There was no room at the Inn. Mary and Joseph stayed in the stable.

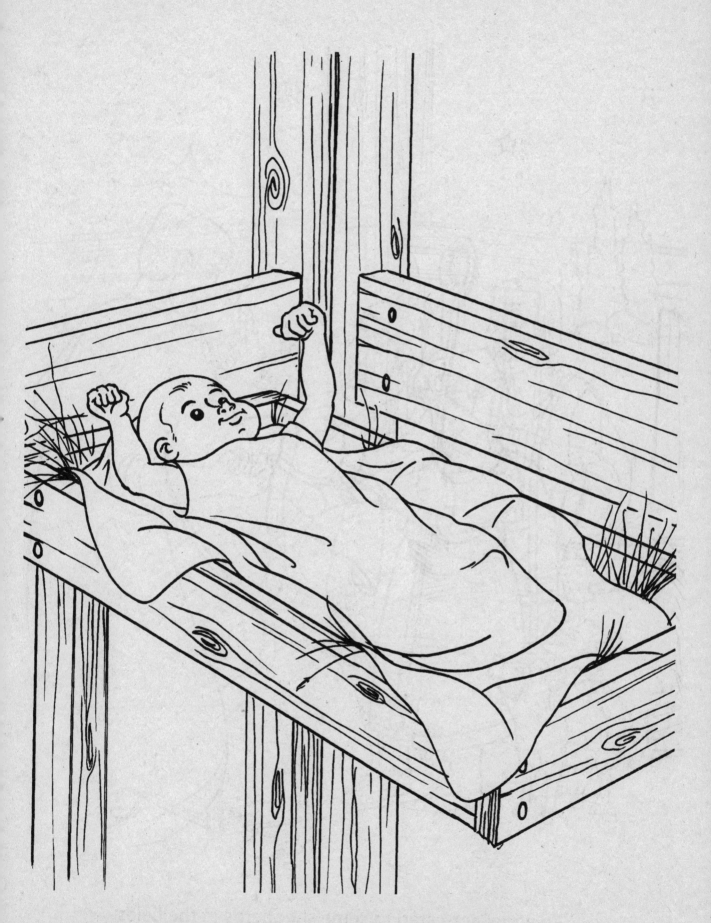

While they were there, Mary had her baby and called him Jesus.

An angel appeared to some shepherds in the fields
and told them of the birth.

The shepherds went to see Jesus and spread the news of his birth.

Later, wise men from Jerusalem came looking for the child.

King Herod told the wise men to return and tell him where the child could be found.

The wise men followed a star in the east.

In a dream the wise men were warned not to return to Herod
because he wanted the child dead

The wise men found the young Jesus and presented him gifts.

King Herod was angry that the Messiah had been born.

An angel warned Joseph and his family to flee to Egypt.

King Herod ordered all male children under the age of two
to be put to death.

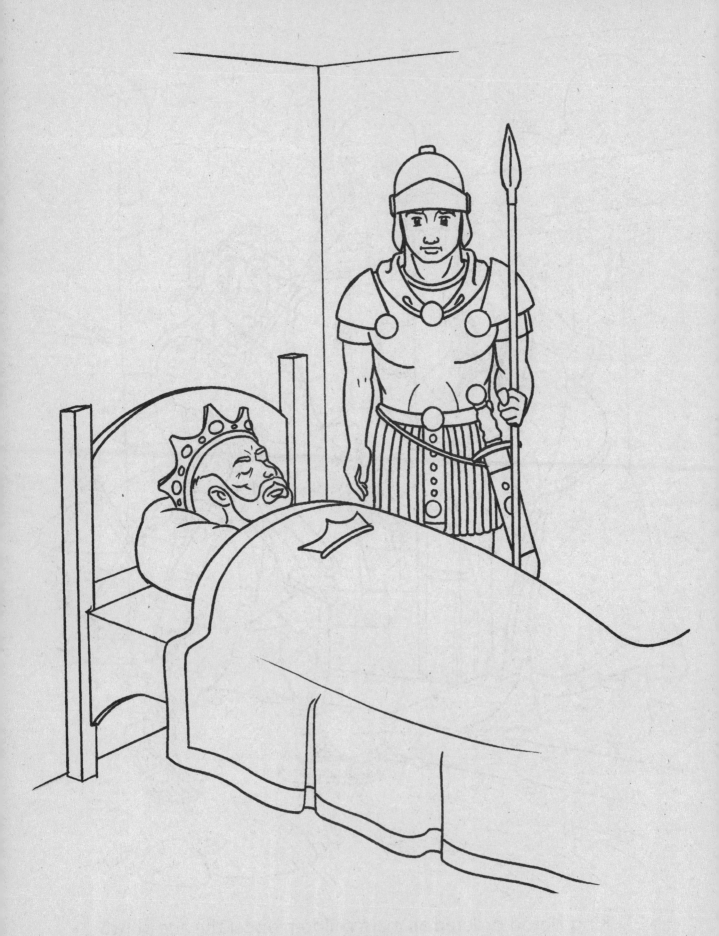

Years later, the evil King Herod died.

After Herod's death, Joseph, Mary, and Jesus returned to Nazareth.

Jesus stayed behind in the Temple on a trip home from Jerusalem.

Joseph and Mary found him in the Temple talking with teachers.

"Did you not know that I must be about my Fathers business?"
Jesus said to them.

Jesus grew up, was very wise, and found favor with God.

Jesus was baptized by John the Baptist.

God speaks, "You are beloved son; In You I am well pleased.

Jesus went into the wilderness to be tempted by the devil for forty days.

After forty days of not eating, the devil tempted Jesus to
turn stones into bread.

"Man shall not live by bread alone, but by every word of God".

The devil offered Jesus all He could see if He would worship him.

You shall worship the Lord your God and Him only shall you serve".

The devil told Jesus to throw Himself off the mountain top and call upon the angels to save Him.

"You shall not tempt the Lord your God"; and so Jesus overcame the devil.

Jesus began His Ministry when He was thirty years old.

His first disciples were Andrew and Peter.

then, Philip and Nathanael.

He also called James and John to be His disciples.

Jesus and His disciples were invited to a wedding festival.

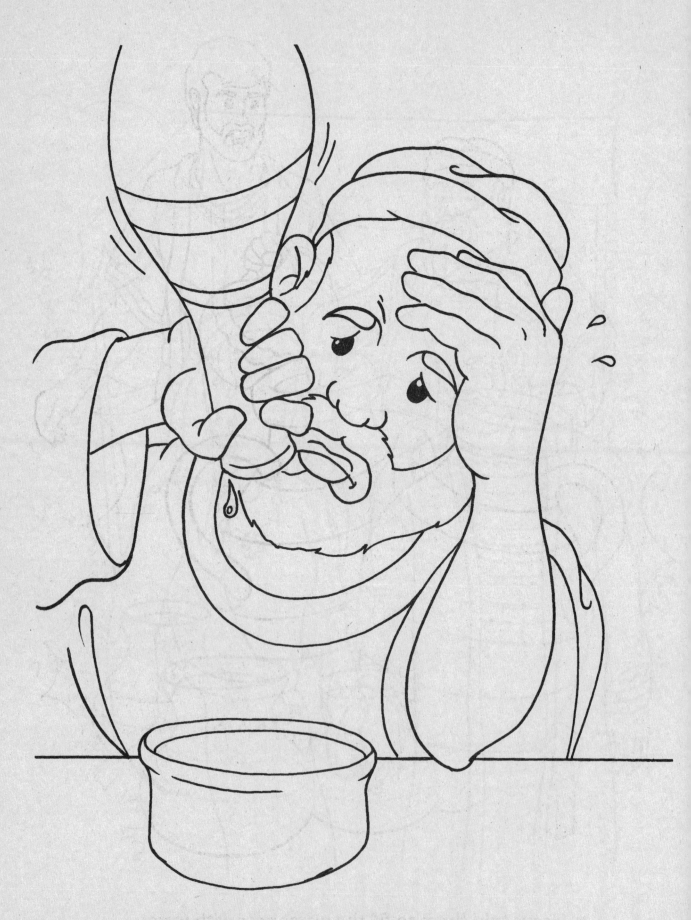

During the wedding the host ran out of wine.

Jesus told them to fill the water pots with water
and he turned the water into wine.

One day Jesus found found people trading in the Temple.

Jesus tipped over the tables of the money changers.

Jesus healed many people; like the nobleman's son
He healed without even seeing the boy.

Jesus told a paralyzed man, "Arise and walk!" And he did!

Jesus healed a man's withered hand.

Lazarus had been dead for four days. Jesus said, "Lazarus come forth."
And he came out of his tomb.

Jesus called Matthew, a tax collector, to be a disciple.

The other disciples were Thomas, Simon, and Thaddaeus.

and, Bartholomew, James, and Judas Iscariot.

One day a great storm hit the sea where they were sailing.

The disciples were afraid of the storm.

Jesus came up on deck and commanded the wind and water to be calm.

After a day of healing and teaching, a crowd of 5000 people were hungry.

They only had five loafs of bread and two small fish to feed the people.

Jesus blessed the the meal and broke the food into pieces.

After the crowd ate, there were several baskets of leftovers.

One night while the disciples were at sea,
Jesus walked out to the boat to meet them.

Peter got out of the boat to walk out to meet Jesus,
but started to sink into the water.

Jesus reached out his hand to save him, saying, "Oh ye of little faith."

When the time came to pay taxes, Jesus told Peter to go catch a fish.

Peter caught a fish.
In it's mouth was a coin they could use to pay their taxes.

Jesus always blessed little children.

The chief priests did not like Jesus and offered Judas
thirty pieces of silver to betray Him.

On the night of the Passover, Judas betrayed Jesus
in the Garden of Gethsemane.

Jesus was taken prisoner by Roman soldiers.

The high priest Caiaphas accused Jesus of blasphemy
and ordered Him over to Pontius Pilate.

Pontius Pilate found no fault in Jesus and told the people so.

It was a custom at Passover time to release a prisoner.
Pilate asked the crowd who to release, Barabbas or Jesus.

Pilate wanted to release Jesus, but the crowd chose Barabbas.

Jesus was beaten and sentenced to be crucified.

He was forced to carry his own crucifixion stake.

After Jesus was crucified, He was laid to rest in a nearby tomb.

Three days later, Mary came to the tomb.
An angel told her that Jesus had risen.

Jesus told His disciples to preach the Gospel of the Kingdom of God.

Jesus blessed the disciples and ascended into the Heavens.